A Slice THROUGH A City

PETER KENT

MACDONALD YOUNG BOOKS

First published in Great Britian in 1995 by
Macdonald Young Books Ltd
Campus 400
Maylands Avenue
Hemel Hempstead
Hertfordshire
HP2 7EZ

A CIP catalogue for this book is available from
the British Library

ISBN 0 7500 1743 0

Commissioning Editor: Thomas Keegan
Editor: Jill A. Laidlaw
Designer: Simon Borrough
Illustrator: Peter Kent

Printed and bound in Portugal by Ediçoes ASA

CONTENTS

Introduction   8

Treasure Trove   9

The Stone Age   10

The Iron Age   12

The Romans   14

The Dark Ages   16

The Middle Ages   18

The 16th Century   20

The 17th Century   22

The 18th Century   24

The 19th Century   26

The 20th Century   28

INTRODUCTION

When people have lived in the same place for a very long time layers of remains build up as rubbish collects and buildings get knocked down. Underneath our feet lie layers of history with the oldest at the bottom and the newest at the top. If you could dig down through the soil you would find old objects in the different layers of soil. You can tell the date of each layer by the things found buried in it. This book cuts a slice through a city built on a site where people have lived for thousands of years.

The 19th Century
The 18th Century
The 17th Century
The 16th Century
The Middle Ages
The Dark Ages
The Romans
The Iron Age
Stone Age

FOLLOW THE FAMILY

In a very old city it is quite likely that some families have lived there for hundreds of years, sometimes even in the same house.

In the city in this book there is one family who have lived and worked there throughout the ages and if you look carefully you can find them on every page. Sometimes their descendants are rich and sometimes they are quite poor. In every age they have different jobs and wear the fashions of the time. To make them easy to find amongst the teeming city crowds they have red hair.

Here they are in costumes from different ages. The man is wearing the sort of clothes worn in the Iron Age about 200 B.C. The woman is wearing clothes of the Middle Ages, the boy is dressed in the costume of the 17th century and the girl wears 19th century fashion.

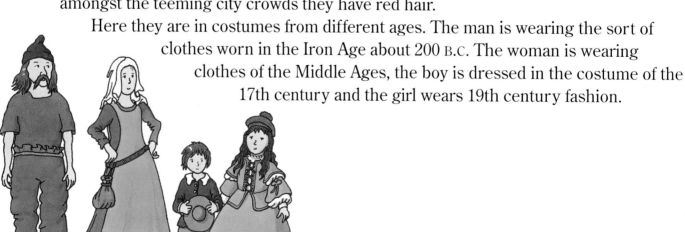

Stone axes from the Stone Age were not always rough and crude. Many were polished and ground to a jewel-like finish.

TREASURE TROVE

It was the fashion in the Middle Ages to have very long and pointed shoes. Some shoes were so long that they had to be tied to the leg with a chain. Shoes then were not made for left and right feet and most had no heels.

The people who dig through the soil to look for remains from our history are called archaeologists. They are very careful when they dig up a site. The place where every object is found, and the objects themselves, are carefully recorded. Photographs are taken and measurements are made.

The things that archaeologists find are very important as they help us to understand how people lived in the past. When a Stone Age woman threw out a broken pot she did not realise that her rubbish would be carefully examined and even glued back together and put on display centuries later.

Even something quite small like a button can tell us a lot about the people who made it. It gives us an idea of what sort of clothes they wore, how skilled they were at making things and, if it is not made of a material found locally, it tells us how far they travelled.

Thousands of objects are buried beneath the city waiting to be dug up, either by accident or by searching archaeologists. If you look carefully through the following city slices you will find all the things on this page.

Pots were very useful for storing food in and eating and drinking from. Stone Age pots were made from clay and decorated with patterns made with wooden combs. They were then baked hard in a kiln.

In the Iron Age people displayed their wealth as jewellery. A rich person would wear magnificent gold necklaces and armlets called torcs.

The Romans were skilled at making statues. They either cut them in stone or cast them in bronze. Some were huge, designed to stand on monuments or in temples, but many were small ornaments for the home.

Tobacco was first brought to Europe from America in the 16th century. It was smoked in pipes made of baked clay. People thought it was good for their health. They even thought that it stopped them catching the plague!

In the 17th century cannons fired solid iron balls. The largest weighed 29 kilograms and were 200 millimetres wide, but 8 kilogram balls were more usual. They are still dug up from old battlefields.

Doctors and pharmacists in the 18th century made their own medicines and sold them in bottles like the one on the right. A blue bottle often meant that the contents were poisonous. Bottled fizzy drinks were popular in the early 19th century. Round-bottomed bottles were stored on their sides to keep the corks moist.

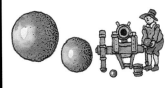

THE STONE AGE

The time over three thousand years ago is called the Stone Age because the tools people used then were made of stone. At the beginning of the Stone Age people travelled around the countryside with their possessions in search of food. During the last part of the Stone Age people learnt how to grow crops and keep animals and so could live in one place. They built simple houses of wood, mud and thatch.

Stone Age people's knives, axes and scrapers were made out of flint. When they could not find enough flint on the ground they dug pits to mine it. Needles and small tools were made out of bone. Deer antlers were used as picks and oxen's shoulder blades as shovels. As stone and bone tools were lost or thrown away they became buried underground. It is the remains of these houses and objects that archaeologists look for today.

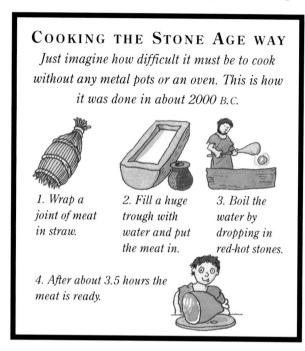

COOKING THE STONE AGE WAY

Just imagine how difficult it must be to cook without any metal pots or an oven. This is how it was done in about 2000 B.C.

1. Wrap a joint of meat in straw.

2. Fill a huge trough with water and put the meat in.

3. Boil the water by dropping in red-hot stones.

4. After about 3.5 hours the meat is ready.

STONE CIRCLES

The greatest monuments of the Stone Age are the stone circles. We do not know the real purpose of these mysterious stones but they were probably like giant calendars marking the seasons and religious festivals.

At a stone circle in Avebury a skeleton was found under one of the fallen stones. It was the remains of a 17th-century farmer. He was trying to break up the stone when it toppled over and crushed him.

THE IRON AGE

In about 2000 B.C. people discovered how to make tools out of metal. At first they used copper but this was very soft. Then they learned how to mix tin with copper to make bronze, which was harder. In about 800 B.C. people began to make tools and weapons out of iron which was the strongest metal of them all.

Iron Age towns were often protected by strong walls made of timber and earth. Houses were larger and more comfortable than they were during the Stone Age. People had learned by now how to weave cloth and make beautiful jewellery in gold and silver. They sold their goods outside their town, and also bought goods from distant places. Money was used for the first time instead of swapping goods. Iron bars were used as money at first but later they were replaced by gold coins.

BLUE TATTOOS

The people of the Iron Age painted or tattooed themselves with intricate swirling patterns drawn in a blue vegetable dye called woad.

WAR CHARIOTS

Chariots were used in Iron Age warfare. Warriors ran down the harness pole of the chariot as it was driven at full speed ready to fight their enemies.

THE ROMANS

By about A.D. 100 the mighty Romans had conquered most of Europe and made it part of their vast empire. The Romans put up the first buildings in brick and stone in what is now Britain and France.

A Roman town had a central market and meeting place called a forum, a town hall, many shops, paved streets and public baths with hot water and central heating. The bigger towns had several temples, and an amphitheatre where games and fights between gladiators took place.

The Romans knew that clean people are healthier and they built proper sewers and organised a good supply of fresh water into towns.

SMELLY POTS

Although the Romans were keen on keeping clean, their blocks of flats (bottom left) must have been very smelly. There were no toilets and urine was collected in great big pots at the bottom of the stairs. The urine was then sold to clothmakers who used it to stiffen fabric.

WAITING FOR WATER

Only the richest houses had water piped directly into them. Most people got their water from public fountains. These must have been very social places where people gossipped as they queued.

HOUSEHOLD GODS

Every Roman home had a shrine and an altar dedicated to the household gods, called the Lares. The head of the family made an offering there every day to keep in favour with the gods.

KEEPING OUT BURGLARS

The Romans did not have a proper police force and were worried about being burgled. They built their houses with only a few windows on the walls facing the street and fitted doors with complicated locks. In many houses the door was jammed shut with a pole.

THE DARK AGES

In the fifth century A.D. the Roman Empire, which had been growing weaker for a century, was invaded by barbarian tribes from northern Europe. The barbarian tribes that settled within the old Empire — the Goths, Franks and Saxons — did not want to live in the Roman towns and the buildings quickly fell into ruin.

The barbarians could not build with stone at first and their houses were usually made of wood with thatched roofs. The most important building in any village was the hall of the chief or 'Thegn' where he lived with his warriors.

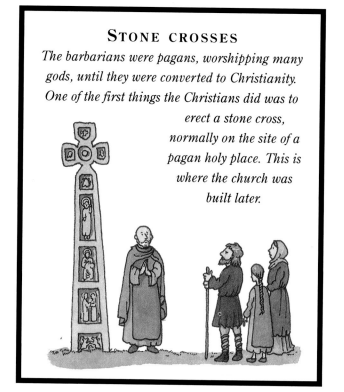

STONE CROSSES

The barbarians were pagans, worshipping many gods, until they were converted to Christianity. One of the first things the Christians did was to erect a stone cross, normally on the site of a pagan holy place. This is where the church was built later.

LEARNING TO BUILD

When the Franks and the Saxons began to build in stone in about A.D. 700 they copied the Roman ruins around them. As you can see from this picture, their first efforts were very clumsy.

SAXON TREASURE

The Saxons were skilled jewellery makers. Wealthy men and women wore splendid brooches, clasps and pendants. These were often made of gold and decorated with glass or coloured stones.

THE MIDDLE AGES

Uring the Middle Ages (roughly 1000 to 1500) towns grew and became rich again. Over much of Europe the houses were made of wooden frames with plaster walls. Only castles, churches and the houses of the very wealthy were built of stone. The streets were often unpaved, with open drains, and it was difficult to keep the town clean. Animals wandered about and people threw rubbish out of their windows.

The market place was very important. People came in from the country to sell food and buy goods made in the town. Shops were simple rooms that opened out on to the street. Almost all of the things people sold in them were made in the house behind.

KEEPING WARM

Most poor people had no fireplaces in their houses. They kept warm by an open fire in a metal grill.

MIRACLE PLAYS

People were very religious during the Middle Ages and celebrated holy days with feasts and festivals. Miracle plays, performed in the street, were popular religious plays and groups of townsfolk would club together to put on a particular scene.

FOOTBALL

A favourite street entertainment was football. Sometimes hundreds played in one game! It was noisy and dangerous — houses were damaged and people killed.

THE 16TH CENTURY

By the 16th century houses were larger and had chimneys instead of just a hole in the roof. Most windows were filled with glass for the first time instead of being closed with wooden shutters. Although still built mainly from wood, houses were more comfortable and contained more furniture and ornaments.

The city streets were still unpaved, dirty and littered with rubbish. At night the city was dark and often dangerous. Fresh water was taken to houses by a person who worked as a water-carrier or fetched by the family from a fountain (unless a house had a well). There were no proper drains and during the summer the city was very smelly and unhealthy.

PUBLIC PUNISHMENT
Criminals were often whipped through the streets, or put in the stocks to have rotten vegetables thrown at them.

STREET ENTERTAINMENT
Entertainers such as musicians, jugglers and people with performing animals earned their living by putting on shows in the streets.

THE 17TH CENTURY

Very few cities survived the 17th century without being wholly or partly destroyed by a fire. Often the cause was accidental but many cities were burnt down after being bombarded or captured by enemies. Soldiers who captured cities also badly damaged them as they searched every house for things to steal.

Outbreaks of plague killed thousands of people. The plague was mainly spread by rats who made their nests in the wooden houses and fed on the rubbish that lay in the streets.

FIRE FIGHTING
Long hooks pulled burning thatch off roofs. Fire engines were just hand-pumps.

MELTING ROOFS
Churches had roofs made out of lead. In a fire this melted and filled the gutters with bright streams of boiling, splashing, molten lead.

PLAGUE PITS

So many people died from the plague that they were buried together in huge pits.

THE 18TH CENTURY

The great fires of the 17th century meant that many cities were almost completely rebuilt in the 18th century. Most of the old wooden buildings were replaced by houses built in brick and stone. This new style of architecture was based on copies of Roman buildings. Streets were properly paved and parts of the city began to be less cramped as wide streets and broad squares were built.

SEDAN CHAIRS
Wealthy people took a sedan chair through crowded city streets. These could be hired like taxis today.

WATCHMEN

There was still no police force in cities. The streets were patrolled by watchmen. A popular sport for young men was knocking over the watchman's shelter and rolling him along the street in it!

FIRE BRIGADES

Iron plates told the private fire brigades that a house was insured with their Fire Assurance Company. If the house wasn't insured with their company they let it burn down.

5537

THE 19TH CENTURY

During the 19th century cities changed more than at any other time in their history. They grew much larger and all sorts of different buildings were constructed. There were railway stations, concert halls, libraries, offices and schools. The streets were properly paved and brightly lit by gas lamps. Underground pipes carried gas and water into the city and sewage out of the city. Cities became healthier and less smelly places to live in, but they suffered from a new problem — traffic jams!

CROSSING SWEEPERS

The streets were covered with horse droppings, mud and rubbish. Poor children earned a little money by sweeping a path across the road for rich people so that they could cross without dirtying their expensive clothes.

STREET LIGHTS

As evening fell men called lamplighters made their way along the streets with a flame on the end of a long pole, lighting the public gas lamps.

10

THE 20TH CENTURY

During this century wars and rebuilding have destroyed many old buildings. Some of those that remain have been altered to suit new uses. Below the streets more tunnels carry extra drains and electricity, telephone and television cables. Some cities have a public railway

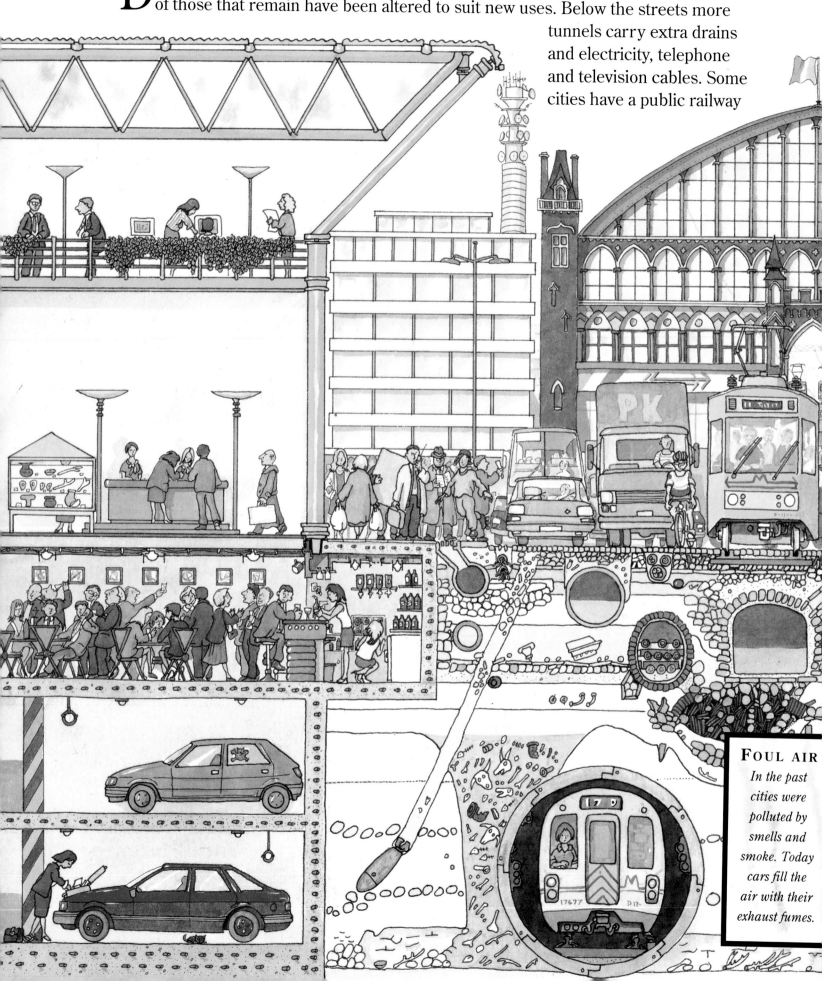

FOUL AIR
In the past cities were polluted by smells and smoke. Today cars fill the air with their exhaust fumes.

system deep underground in tunnels.
Many buildings now rise to great
heights. They have deep foundations to
support their weight. Builders digging
these foundations sometimes help
archaeologists by finding ancient
remains in the oldest parts of cities.

VIDEO POLICEMEN

*Many cities now have
video cameras scanning
the streets. These help to
stop crime.*